GOING
PRO

BECOMING A PRO
BASEBALL
PLAYER

BY ANDREW PINA

Gareth Stevens
PUBLISHING

Please visit our website, www.garethstevens.com. For a free color catalog of all our high-quality books, call toll free 1-800-542-2595 or fax 1-877-542-2596.

Library of Congress Cataloging-in-Publication Data

Pina, Andrew.
Becoming a pro baseball player / by Andrew Pina.
p. cm. — (Going pro)
Includes index.
ISBN 978-1-4824-2054-8 (pbk.)
ISBN 978-1-4824-2053-1 (6-pack)
ISBN 978-1-4824-2055-5 (library binding)
1. Baseball — Juvenile literature. 2. Baseball players — Juvenile literature. I. Title.
GV867.5 P56 2015
796.357—d23

First Edition

Published in 2015 by
Gareth Stevens Publishing
111 East 14th Street, Suite 349
New York, NY 10003

Copyright © 2015 Gareth Stevens Publishing

Designer: Nicholas Domiano
Editor: Therese Shea

Photo credits: Cover, p. 1 peepo/Vetta/Getty Images; p. 5 David Maxwell/Getty Images Sport/Getty Images; p. 7 Michael Zagaris/Getty Images Sport/Getty Images; p. 9 © iStockphoto.com/nicolesy; pp. 11, 29 (background image: baseball diamond) Ben Carlson/Shutterstock.com; pp. 11, 29 (baseball diamond vector) vitamind/Shutterstock.com; p. 12 Al Messerschmidt/Shutterstock.com; p. 13 Christian Petersen/Getty Images Sport/Getty Images; pp. 15, 28 Jamie Squire/Getty Images Sport/Getty Images; p. 17 Justin Edmonds/Getty Images Sport/Getty Images; p. 18 Maddie Meyer/Getty Images Sport/Getty Images; p. 19 Norm Hall/Getty Images Sport/Getty Images; pp. 20, 21 Rob Carr/Getty Images Sport/Getty Images; p. 23 Paige Calamari/Major League Baseball/Getty Images; p. 24 Ezra Shaw/Getty Images Sport/Getty Images; p. 25 Brace Hemmelgarn/Getty Images Sport/Getty Images; p. 26 Debby Wong/Shutterstock.com; p. 27 Diamond Images/Getty Images.

Printed in the United States of America

CPSIA compliance information: Batch #CW15GS: For further information contact Gareth Stevens, New York, New York at 1-800-542-2595.

CONTENTS

Words in the glossary appear in **bold** type the first time they are used in the text.

UNDERSTAND THE BASICS

Standing at home plate in Boston's Fenway Park with 37,000 screaming fans, David Ortiz of the Red Sox has a lot of pressure on his shoulders to hit a home run. Every baseball player wants to score a run in the game, but players in the **pros** usually have to work very hard before they can smack the ball over the fence. They all started with the basics years before they got the chance to make a big play.

The three main parts of baseball are hitting, **fielding**, and pitching. Each of these requires different skills, but all are important to creating a great baseball team.

MANY PATHS

The path to a professional baseball career depends on where you're from. Baseball is played all over the world. There are professional baseball leagues in Asia, Australia, Europe, North America, and South America. Countries in all these places have players who end up in Major League Baseball (MLB) in the United States and Canada.

David Ortiz, or "Big Papi," is a designated hitter. That's a player who usually doesn't play defense but bats in place of the pitcher.

STEP UP TO THE PLATE

The bat head is the thickest part of the baseball bat and produces the most power. Pros have learned how to keep their eye on the ball while training their brain to know where the bat head is without looking at it. Hitting well takes a lot of practice and patience as they're both needed to win a game.

At first, many players practice hitting a baseball off a **batting tee**. The tee isn't just for kids; adults use batting tees, too. Since the ball isn't moving on the tee, it's easy to keep your eye on it. A tee can help you learn where the bat head is when you swing.

SWINGING HARD VS. SOLID CONTACT

A hard swing that hits the ball with the narrow part of the bat won't go very far. A softer swing that hits with the solid part of the bat can go farther. A good batter understands swinging hard isn't as important as making solid contact.

Batting tees are perfect for practicing your swing. However, in a real game, batters have to wait for the right pitch to hit it out of the park.

Soft-toss baseball drills, or exercises, are another good batting practice. The pitcher sits or stands a few feet away and tosses the ball softly to the batter. This way, the batter can work on their timing. They'll easily see the ball go up and come down, and can time their swing to make good contact.

Next, batters must have regular batting practice. A coach or a pitcher stands on the mound and throws pitches into the strike zone, or the area over the plate and between the batter's armpits and knees. Pitches like these are key for making solid contact with the ball.

LEGS = POWER!

If you reach up with your arms, you can only reach so high. But if you jump, you can reach higher. It's similar with swinging a bat. If you only use your arms, you're forgetting about your legs. If you position and use your legs correctly, extra power is released into your swing.

Players may also use batting cages with pitching machines to practice hitting.

GET DEFENSIVE

Unlike in sports such as basketball and soccer, baseball players don't move quickly from offense to defense and back again. Instead, baseball teams take turns on offense and defense. They're two separate—but equally important—parts of the game. Both offensive and defensive skills should be practiced to become a well-rounded player.

How a player trains for defense depends on what position they play. Position players are the players who don't pitch. They play in the infield (on the dirt near the bases) or in the outfield (on the grass beyond the infield). All positions are key to keeping the opposing team from scoring.

DID YOU KNOW?

Baseball is one of the few sports where the offense never has the ball. Instead, the defense has the ball most of the time. The batter attempts to score by hitting the ball away from the defense and getting runners across home plate. A runner who touches the baseball after it's been hit is out!

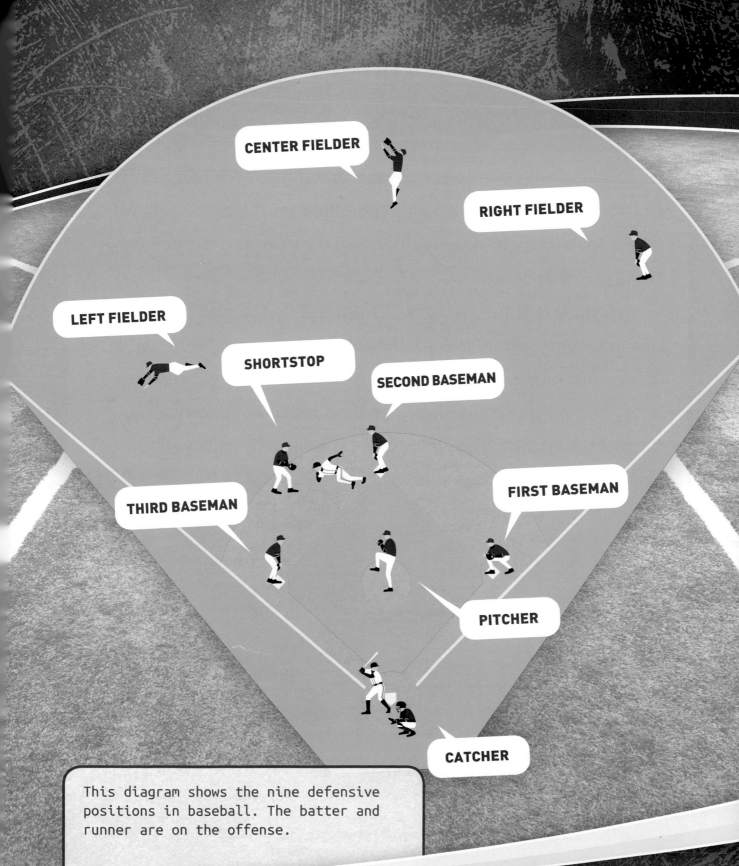

This diagram shows the nine defensive positions in baseball. The batter and runner are on the offense.

Infielders have to be able to catch a ball or recover a ball rolling along the ground. Then they must get the ball from their glove to their throwing hand and throw it to a base all in a matter of seconds.

In one drill for infielders, a batter hits the ball along the ground. While an infielder is fielding the ball, the batter yells "1" for first base, "2" for second base, "3" for third base, or "4" for home plate. The infielder then repositions to quickly throw to the base. This drill helps an infielder improve the skills needed to stop a runner from getting on base.

CATCHER

Catcher is perhaps the hardest defensive position for many reasons. Catchers suggest pitches and must have an **accurate** throwing arm. They also must have strong legs. Every time the ball is pitched, the catcher squats, or bends at the knees so they're almost sitting on their heels. A catcher squats around 150 times per game!

Making one play sometimes isn't enough for an infielder. Dee Gordon of the Los Angeles Dodgers throws to another infielder to get a second runner out.

OUTFIELD

A baseball can move **unpredictably** through the air because of the spin on the ball and the wind. One way to practice tracking and catching a soaring baseball is to catch balls during batting practice.

Outfielders not only need to throw the ball a long distance, but they also have to throw it accurately to get it to the right person in time. To practice an accurate throw, hold the ball in your glove in the middle of your chest. Point your shoulder, elbow, and foot on your gloved side at your target. While throwing the ball, bring your chest to your glove and swing your back foot forward.

BARREL TOSS

One way to get an accurate throwing arm is to do a barrel toss. Position an open container at home plate and stand in the outfield. Try to get the ball into the container by throwing it directly in or bouncing it on the ground first. This **mimics** throwing home to the catcher.

An outfielder often needs to reposition to make sure they're right under the falling ball.

ON THE MOUND

Pitchers need to be accurate, fast throwers from a short distance. They need to build great arm strength to pitch well throughout a game. And just like infielders, pitchers also have to sometimes field balls on the ground. So, infield practice is important for them, too.

One pitching drill is called the bucket drill. Right-handed pitchers kneel on their right knee and put the top of their right foot on an upside-down bucket. They place their left foot on the ground in front of them. The pitcher throws the ball and pops up on their left foot as they complete the power-producing throwing motion.

AVOID OVEREXERTION

Resting a pitcher's arm is essential for a long career. Pitchers should warm up and stretch before throwing. They shouldn't overexert their arms, or throw too much or too hard. Pitchers shouldn't experience pain when they throw. It's not unusual for an MLB pitcher to "blow out," or greatly injure, their arm.

It takes years for a pro pitcher to perfect his throwing style. Here, Clayton Kershaw of the Los Angeles Dodgers hurls a pitch over home plate.

STAY FLEXIBLE

Being **flexible** isn't only for gymnasts! In baseball, there are many **repetitive** activities. In each game, a batter might take 20 swings or more. A pitcher might throw 100 pitches a game. Being flexible helps these players' muscles make the same motions over and over without getting hurt. Before practice and games, coaches or trainers lead players through stretches.

Here's an effective stretch before the game: Sit on the ground with your legs apart. Next, bend at the waist, touch one foot, then the other foot, and finally bend forward as far as comfortable. These movements stretch almost every part of the body!

TIM LINCECUM

Even though he's only 5 feet 11 inches (180 cm) tall, Tim Lincecum produces as much speed on his fastball as taller pitchers. That's because he's so flexible. In fact, his **stride** toward home plate is 30 percent longer than his height, while many pitchers have a stride 20 percent shorter than their height.

Professional trainers teach teams the most important stretches to prevent injury in their sport.

AMATEUR BASEBALL

Most young players start baseball in youth leagues, such as Little League. Little League has many levels, from Tee Ball for children 4 to 7 years old all the way up to Big League for teenagers. For children 11 to 13 years old, the best teams from each region of the United States and around the world play in the Little League World Series every year in South Williamsport, Pennsylvania.

Many young people also have the opportunity to play baseball on their school team in elementary, junior high, and high school. They may compete as well on traveling teams and American Legion teams, which mostly play games around their region and state.

A REAL TRAVEL TEAM

Did you know that baseball is played in Africa? In 2012, a Little League team from Lugazi, Uganda, made it all the way to the Little League World Series in South Williamsport, Pennsylvania. It was the first time an African team made it that far.

Little League action can be as exciting as the MLB!

IN NORTH AMERICA

Even if they never make it to the Little League World Series, **amateur** baseball players from the United States, Canada, and Puerto Rico have opportunities in high school and college to get noticed by professional **scouts**. These scouts attend games at both levels and are responsible for recommending players to Major League Baseball teams. The teams can then choose the player during the draft, the event in which teams select amateur players to play for their organization.

Players can be drafted after their senior year of high school, during community or junior college, or after they turn 21 while attending a 4-year college. Drafted players are usually placed in the minor leagues at first.

INTERNATIONAL PLAYERS

Baseball players outside the United States and Canada follow different rules when signing with teams. International players may sign with MLB teams when they're as young as 16 or 17, depending on their birth date and whether they're in school. Pro players in Japan and Korea can be released from their team there if an MLB team pays their team enough money.

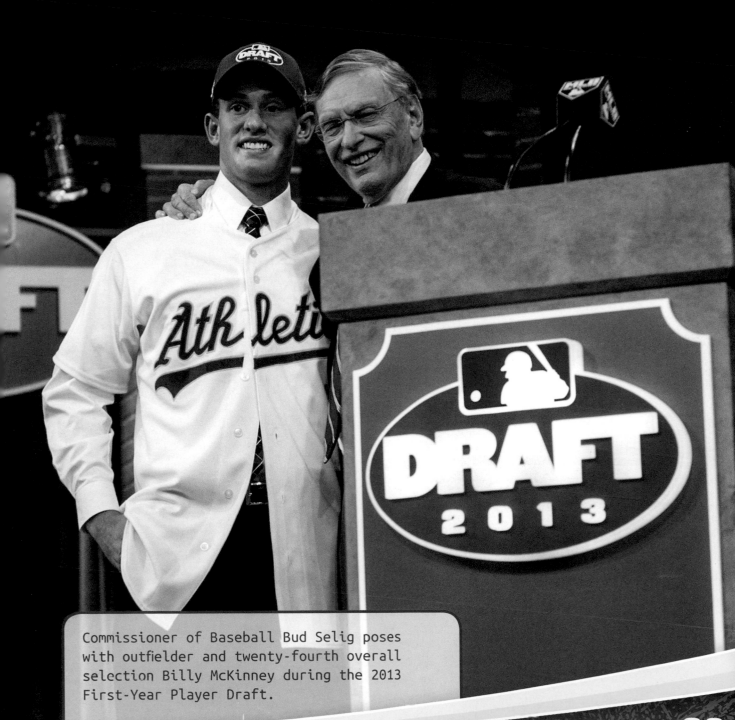

Commissioner of Baseball Bud Selig poses
with outfielder and twenty-fourth overall
selection Billy McKinney during the 2013
First-Year Player Draft.

HIGH SCHOOL OR COLLEGE?

An excellent player on a high school or traveling team may be drafted by an MLB team after high school. Sometimes, though, a player can improve their skills, and therefore draft position, by attending college and playing on the college's baseball team. And if the player gets a **scholarship**, they may be able to attend the college at little or no cost.

Improving draft position can make a big financial difference. A player can receive extra money, called a signing bonus, when signing an MLB contract. If the player has a good draft position, the signing bonus could be worth thousands, or even millions, of dollars.

BUSTER POSEY

After Buster Posey finished high school in 2005, he was drafted in the fiftieth round by the Los Angeles Angels of Anaheim. He chose to go to college instead, and after finishing college, he was selected fifth overall in the first round of the 2008 draft by the San Francisco Giants. He signed a **lucrative** contract with a $6.2 million signing bonus!

Minnesota Twins 2013 first-round draft pick Kohl Stewart signs his contract on June 19, 2013, in Minnesota.

MINOR LEAGUES

Most pros start their career in the minor leagues, or "farm system." Rookie League is the lowest level. It's mostly for players in their first or second year of pro ball. If they do well there, they move up to Single A (A), Double A (AA), or Triple A (AAA). Each MLB team usually has one AAA team, one AA team, and often more than one Rookie and A team.

An MLB team needs its farm system to build skills in players who aren't prepared for the big leagues. A minor league team also provides pros a chance to get ready to return to the major leagues after an injury.

LEVELING THE TALENT

Some players experience all levels of the minor leagues. Others may be moved straight from AA to the majors. That happened to outfielder Mike Trout (above) when he was just 19. AAA baseball has a mix of younger players and older players who may have played in the majors. Some minor league baseball players never reach the majors.

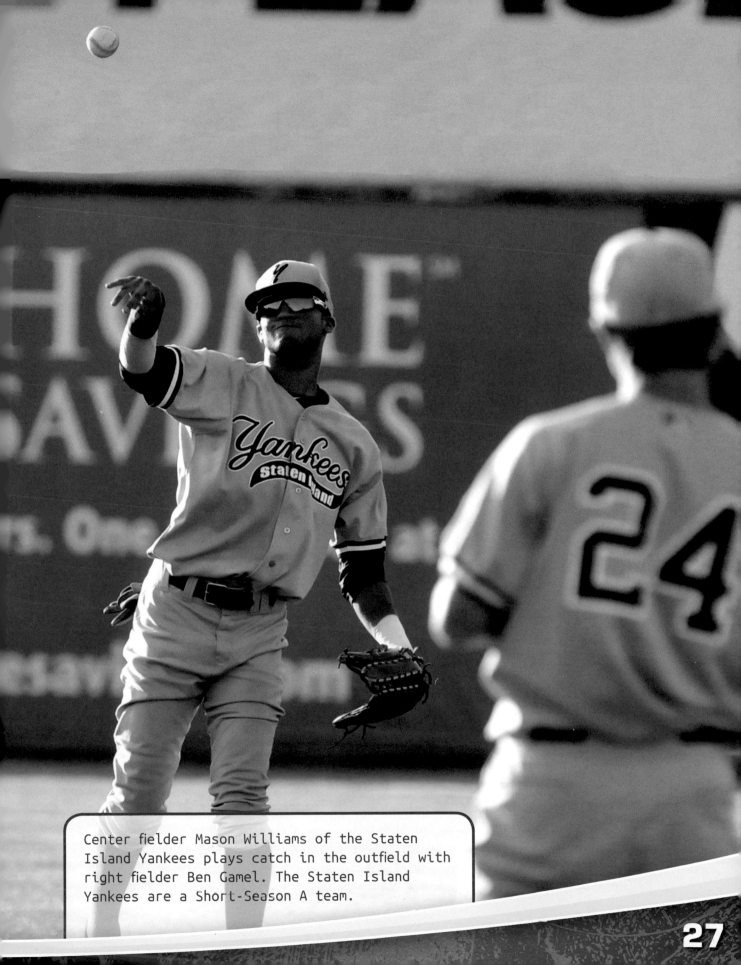

Center fielder Mason Williams of the Staten Island Yankees plays catch in the outfield with right fielder Ben Gamel. The Staten Island Yankees are a Short-Season A team.

FINALLY IN THE MAJORS

It's unusual for players to go from the draft straight to an MLB team, though some zoom through the minors. Other players, like pitcher R. A. Dickey, bounce between the minors and majors before establishing themselves in the MLB. Players from overseas, such as outfielder Yasiel Puig from Cuba or pitcher Yu Darvish from Japan, might play a long time in their home countries before coming to the US major leagues.

All players have to put in an incredible amount of work before they make it big. However, once you make it to the major leagues, you can be proud you're one of the best baseball players in the world.

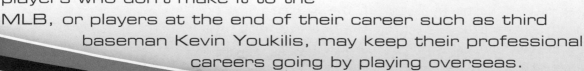

BOSTON RED SOX

OTHER MAJOR LEAGUES

There are baseball major leagues in other countries, too, such as Japan, Mexico, and South Korea. American players who don't make it to the MLB, or players at the end of their career such as third baseman Kevin Youkilis, may keep their professional careers going by playing overseas.

MAKING THE MAJORS

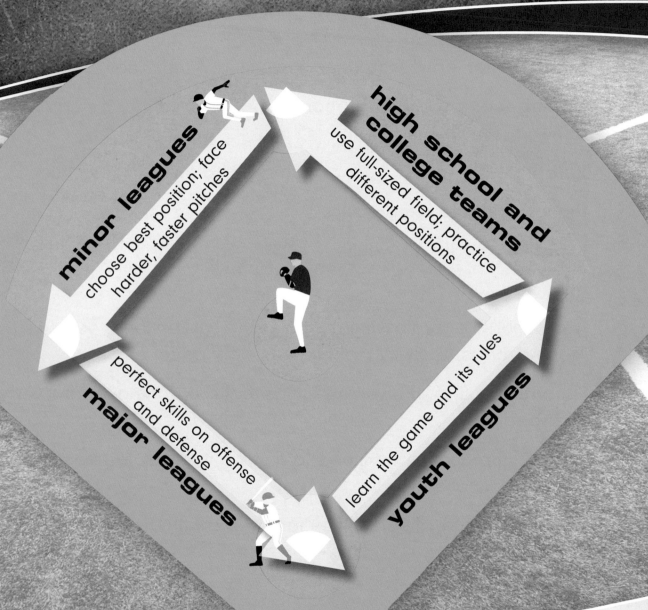

high school and college teams
use full-sized field; practice different positions

minor leagues
choose best position; face harder, faster pitches

major leagues
perfect skills on offense and defense

youth leagues
learn the game and its rules

GLOSSARY

accurate: free from mistakes

amateur: someone who does something without pay

batting tee: a tool that supports a baseball so that it's easier to hit

field: to recover, pick up, or catch a ball after it's been struck

flexible: able to bend easily

lucrative: producing wealth

mimic: to copy closely

pros: short for "professional leagues." A professional earns money from an activity that many people do for fun.

repetitive: full of or involving things that are done over and over again

scholarship: money awarded to a student to pay for their college education

scout: someone who searches for people with great skills in a sport

stride: a long step

unpredictably: acting in a manner so that it's hard to guess what will happen in the future

FOR MORE INFORMATION

Books

Franks, Katie. *I Want to Be a Baseball Player.* New York, NY: PowerKids Press, 2007.

Gifford, Clive. *Baseball.* New York, NY: Marshall Cavendish Benchmark, 2010.

Stanley, Glen F., and Jason Porterfield. *An Insider's Guide to Baseball.* New York, NY: Rosen Central, 2015.

Websites

Baseball-Reference.com
baseball-reference.com
Find everything you want to know about Major League Baseball, including facts, figures, awards, and more.

The Official Site of Minor League Baseball
milb.com
Find out more about your local minor league team.

INDEX